T0384416

Ian Ritchie L I G H T

It takes only one beam of sunlight
to reveal the dust in the air.

UNICORN

Ian Ritchie leads ritchie*studio, one of the world's most innovative and influential contemporary architectural practices, based in London.

He also co-founded the design engineering practice Rice Francis Ritchie (aka RFR) in Paris which contributed to several of President Mitterrand's 'Grands Projets' – Louvre Pyramids and Sculpture Courts, Cité des Sciences and Parc de la Villette, Opéra Bastille, and La Grande Arche de La Défense.

Ian is a Royal Academician and a member of the Akademie der Künste in Berlin. He is Honorary Visiting Professor of Architecture Liverpool University; Fellow of the Society of Façade Engineering and Emeritus Commissioner CABE.

He has been adviser to the British Museum, The Ove Arup Foundation and the Centre for Urban Science and Progress NYU. He has chaired international juries including RIBA Stirling Prize, Czech Architecture Grand Prix and the Berlin Art Prize.

As well as an architect, he is a writer, a poet, and his art is held in several international galleries and museums.

Alba di Milano (Dawn of Milan)

Alba is an arc, so subtle it is almost imperceptible.
The desire of man to reach the heavens asks man
    to overcome the arc.
This escaping arc that simply manifests gravity,
    whether through the solid arrow from a bow,
    or curving water falling from a spout,
    or a luminous November rocket fading away,
    has held us entranced for centuries.
Man eventually made it, but now we ask for what
    purpose.
To escape the earthly mess we have created here,
    and take these human values somewhere else.
Humankind's lifeboat may exist one day,
    and find new water upon which to float and drink
    thanks to the diminished arc,
    But the future may deem that we simply
    changed a letter.
Arc for Ark, and another myth for man.

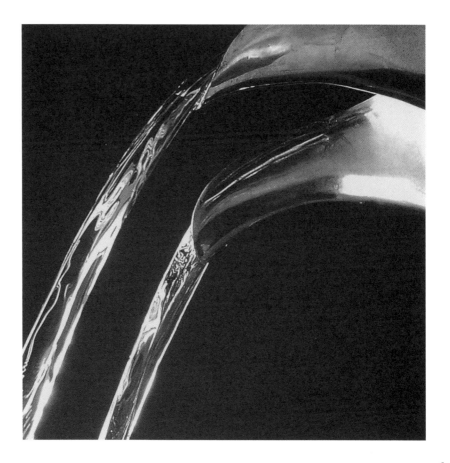

The 'Lotus Effect'

Was the 'Lotus Effect' noticed a long time
    ago, by a tear-eyed lover lying in the
    snow, or a poet by a lake.

The 'Lotus Effect', was seen by twentieth
    century man, electron microscope.
    to hand, who then ran to file a global
    patent.

The 'Lotus Effect', was, like so many
    discoveries, first seen through a
    sharp lens, a mist in the breeze distilled
    on a leaf.

So, if the light of the moon can dance and
    roll on water as dew upon a leaf, a child
    will wonder forever at such beauty.

Trembling droplet, roll easy, from grey
    cloud to deep blue sea, on leaves of jade
    green, as the wind through the tree, and
    sing as you remind us of love's purity.

And then to roll free as the sun lifts us
    from our night's dream.

'Try though we may to split light into fundamental atomic pieces, it remains whole to the end. Our very notion of what it means to be elementary is challenged. Until now we have equated smallest with most fundamental. Perhaps for light, at least, the most fundamental feature is not to be found in smallness, but rather in wholeness, its incorrigible capacity to be one and many, particle and wave, a single thing with the universe inside.'

Arthur Zajonc, *Catching the Light:*
The Entwined History of Light and Mind
(New York: Oxford University Press)

Introduction

We are bathed in light, but we can only perceive light
when it enters our eyes directly, either emanating from a
source or when reflected off a surface. In the vastness of
outer space, the sun's light is everywhere yet falls on nothing;
there is only darkness.

Conversely, we know our surroundings are there, see them,
because they are reflecting ambient light – light literally
summons the world into view. Yet learning to see,
transforming raw sensation into meaningful perception,
is a developmental process, just like learning language.[1]
We actively participate in sight, as our minds are subtly
and continuously forming and re-forming the world we see,
blurring the line between physiology and psychology, science
and philosophy, and giving the lie to the neo-Cartesian
inheritance that treats body and mind as separate entities.

Visible light is only a tiny portion of the total
electromagnetic spectrum, which includes radio waves,
microwaves, infrared radiation, ultraviolet rays, X-rays and

gamma rays, all imperceptible to human eyes (although some animals can see into the infrared or ultraviolet spectrum). Like visible light, these are composed of a stream of massless, discrete packets of energy called photons, travelling in wavelike patterns of varying frequencies and wavelengths. A comprehensive explanation of this wave-particle duality, called quantum electrodynamics (QED), has only existed since the 20th century. Yet light's behaviour remains a mystery, even to the physicist Richard Feynman, who won the Nobel Prize in 1965 for the theory's co-discovery.

> ... the price of gaining such an accurate theory has been the erosion of our common sense. We must accept some very bizarre behavior: the amplification and suppression of probabilities, light reflecting from all parts of a mirror, light travelling in paths other than a straight line, photons going faster or slower than the conventional speed of light, electrons going backwards in time, photons suddenly disintegrating into a positron-electron pair, and so on.
>
> Richard Feynman, *QED: The Strange Theory of Light and Matter* (Princeton & Oxford: Princeton University Press)

QED is only the latest answer to the question of light's nature and meaning, which has been asked since the conscious dawn of our species, when night still hid the mysteries and terrors of the unseeable unknown, and our distant ancestors found security and warmth within a flickering circle of firelight. Over the subsequent span of millennia and many civilisations, it has been addressed by religious thinkers, philosophers, artists and, latterly, technicians and scientists, even as light gathered around itself innumerable associations of great power. With its dark twin, shadow, light has come to shape human perceptions and emotions as well as human technologies in almost every field of endeavour. In the process it has become not only one of our most powerful tools, but one of our richest and most versatile linguistic, artistic and mythological metaphors.

Many origin myths begin with light's emergence from a primeval chaos or night, and the world's end with light's disappearance in a final, all-engulfing darkness. Light is associated with creation and becomes a symbol of life, warmth, clarity, and immortality. Darkness is associated with death, the underworld, or chaos, ignorance and evil. When we speak of 'enlightenment' or 'dark thoughts' or we echo these ancient symbolic meanings.

The story of Western culture's architectural search for the mastery of light over darkness is based upon the shape and size of openings and the infill – glass. It is a chronology of the way light enters buildings and reveals the spatial composition and forms within, and how technological advances and embodied philosophical thought are expressed in structures that serve our physical, economic, and spiritual needs.

Beginning in the 13th century, the search reached a seminal point in the middle of the 19th century with the industrial production of sheet glass and Joseph Paxton's Crystal Palace, built entirely of glass panes held within a framework of modular cast iron elements. By the early 20th century glass, and with it, white light, had become an aesthetic in its own right; its crystal transparency symbolising purity, goodness, illumination, rationality, order, and hygiene.

Transparent envelopes accept natural light as it is, with its continuously changing qualities, modifying it spectrally as it passes through glass. Transparency is rarely an architectural composition of light but a dynamic saturation of space – a situation which nearly always requires the control of the quantity of sunlight by shading.

The dramatic increase in the use of glass and other transparent materials to wrap buildings in late 20th and early 21st century Western architecture questions the very significance of shadows. Spreading worldwide, it echoes the exponential growth in the amount of artificial light sources on the earth, resulting in a continuing decline in the zones of shadow and darkness.

Dioptrics, one of the most delightful of sciences, has allowed us to explore the future through the infinitesimal, and the past further back in time than ever before, through the agency of the James Webb telescope's segmented 'eye' that observes the expanding universe. We experience the world here – and out there – through light, and light conjures the atmospheres of our emotional existence, from the 480nm wavelength in the morning sky that triggers our biorhythms to the flickering romantic candle-lit dinner.

In his 1933 classic In Praise of Shadows, the Japanese author Jun'ichirō Tanizaki pointed out the absurdity of greater and greater quantities of light. Instead, he celebrated the delicate and nuanced aspects of everyday life that were rapidly being lost as artificial illumination took over:

> 'The progressive Westerner is determined always to better his lot. From candle to oil lamp, oil lamp to gaslight, gaslight to electric light – his quest for a brighter light never ceases, he spares no pains to eradicate even the minutest shadow.'

For the great architect – working within a profession which is itself a fusion of art and engineering, philosophy and technology – light, both natural and artificial, is the material of architecture, a tool used to shape and animate form, space, material and experience. Such architects' work acknowledges the nature of light and shadow as interconnected and interdependent forces, giving rise to each other and interacting to form a dynamic system. In a very real sense, it embodies some aspects of Eastern philosophies, in which shadow is often seen as an aspect of the dualistic nature of the universe, representing the unseen or unconscious aspects of the self and the world and a natural part of the balance of life.

> A plan of a building should be read like a harmony of spaces in light. Even a space intended to be dark should have just enough light from some mysterious opening to tell us how dark it really is. Each space must be defined by its structure and the character of its natural light.
>
> Louis Kahn

1 www.newyorker.com/tech/annals-of-technology/people-cured-blindness-see

2 www.science.org/content/article/feature-giving-blind-people-sight-illuminates-brain-s-secrets

Light is the opium of the architect and shadow its form.

Sciagraphy – first year architectural student drawing
by Ian Ritchie, 1965

Light is the fundamental material of all architecture.

'Levitas – the third mountain sculpture' is made of 6cm wide strips of
Italian red oak in the form of two connected anticlastic woven open
gridshell structures – a 'double saddle' structure.

Installed 30 08 2019 at Arte Sella sculpture park,
Borgo Valsugana, Autonomous Province of Trento, Italy
– *photo Giacomo Bianchi*

One reading of the history of architecture
is the story of the way light has entered buildings.

Royal Academy of Music, Angela Burgess Recital Hall oculus
– *photo Adam Scott*

Like an object moving through water,
light cuts through shadows
only to leave shadows in its wake.

Sainsbury Wellcome Centre façade
detail of low-iron cast glass
– *photo Eva Menuhin*

Shadows are holes in light.

Two people shadow – *photo Ian Ritchie*

Light drives away darkness but creates shadows in the
process, and these shadows in turn frame the pools of light.

Similar to the uprooted and mobile modern
individual, Berlin is a city rising up out of an
empty space[1], without apparent historical origins or
firm foundation: sitting "upon ground that is still
undeveloped, unstable and perpetually in need of
improvement", *it is literally a city built on sand where
the dust never settles*[2]. Like its restless dwellers, Berlin
"*always becomes and never is*"[3], it is a city of unrest
and perpetual becoming with all its resident themes
of instability and unmet potential.

1   die Stadt scheint *in dem öden Land* völlig frisch und
unverbunden zu beginnen." (Siehe [1], S. 409.)
2   *Einer aus Sumpf, worin Berlin schwimmt, aus Sand,
worauf es gebaut ist.*" (Siehe [1], S. 409.)
3   *Berlin, ein Gebilde, das sozusagen immer nur wird und nie
ist, …*" (Siehe [1], S. 414.)

[1] Bloch, Ernst: Literarische Aufsätze,
Suhrkamp, Frankfurt a.M. 1985.

*("Das Leben wird hier besonders leicht neu.
Auf den ersten Blick ist die Stadt "bodenlos", völlig frisch
und unverbunden. Berlin, ein Gebilde, das sozusagen
immer nur wird und nie ist.")*

Ernst Bloch's 1932 essay, *Berlin, as Viewed from the
Landscape*, (quoted in Durst xvi)

Freedom and Unity Memorial, Four Doors, Berlin
– *etchings Ian Ritchie*

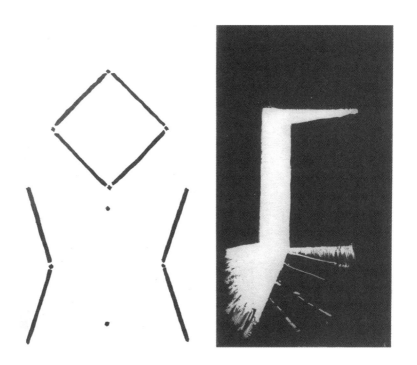

If we allow the natural environment to be the instrument of design at all scales, then our designs will be more intelligent and more responsive to our senses.

Trident Park, Malta, façade detail of solar shading
– *photo Ian Ritchie*

Our perception of spaces and surfaces differs greatly between sunlight and moonlight, artificial light and fire or candlelight.

Royal Academy of Music, Susie Sainsbury Theatre
detail of 'exploded chandelier' auditorium fibre
optic lighting
– *photo Adam Scott*

Our earth is simply the natural greenhouse
of our solar system home.

Light leaving the Earth – *etching Ian Ritchie*

My empathy lies with the lighting designer
who says that the longer we keep the lights switched off
the better we feel and the less energy we use.

Louvre Pyramid – *photo Ian Ritchie*

Beauty is nature's non-linear dance with light.

Moonlight on the Thames at Limehouse, London
– *photo Ian Ritchie*

Sunlight and moonlight move and change space.

Trident Park, Malta, car park detail – *photo Joe Smith*

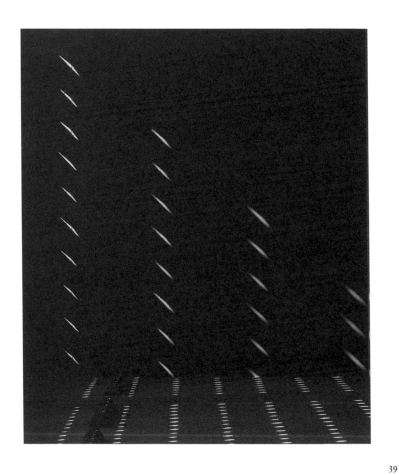

Touching something convinces us of its existence.

Turville Fountain – *etching Ian Ritchie*

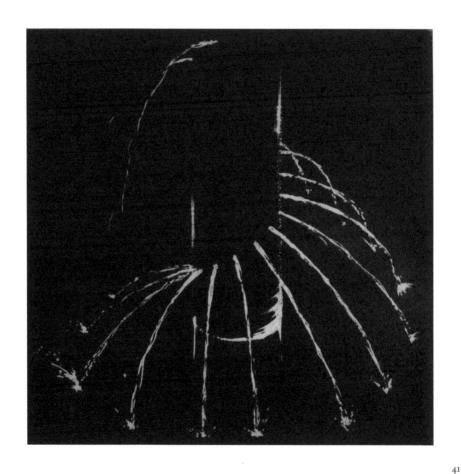

Architecture only comes alive when you're actually there,
and you feel it through your eyes, your nose,
your ears, your feet.

The Brewhouse, Malta – *photo Joe Smith*

Great architecture should connect technology to emotion,
and space to the soul.

Sainsbury Wellcome Centre for Neural Circuits and
Behaviour at UCL colonnade – *photo Eva Menuhin*

Behind every black hole hides a star.

Royal Shakespeare Company 'pebble' theatre
beached at Temple, London – *etching Ian Ritchie*

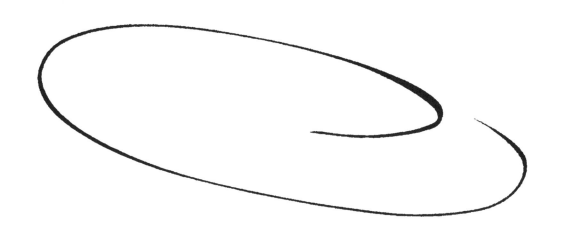

The tree is a weave of light, earth and water.
Nature's perfect architecture – stable, unmoving yet
transforming light into beauty, wind into music,
shade into classroom, leaves into food, twigs into nests …

Crystal Palace Concert Platform – *photo Ian Ritchie*

Like Janus, the architect designs
with history and the future in mind.

Royal Academy of Music concept – *etching Ian Ritchie*

Glass is stone with magical properties.

Louvre Inverted Pyramid – *photo René de Wit*

Architecture holds the unteachable human spirit
aspiring to the unreachable.

Spire of Dublin – *photo Barry Mason*

Leipzig Glass Hall

A framed emptiness
    brings down the sky
    to meet the earth.
Diaphanous shell
    stretched taut over
    squared silhouettes
    of thin round metal.

Light chases darkness.
Shadows are holes
    in light. Colours flow
    throughout the space.
Sunlight and cloud,
    the shadows come
    and go.

Leipzig Glass Hall interior looking east
– *photo Leipziger Messe*

Transparency is simultaneously the negation of light and its totality.

Leipzig silhouette – *drawing Ian Ritchie*

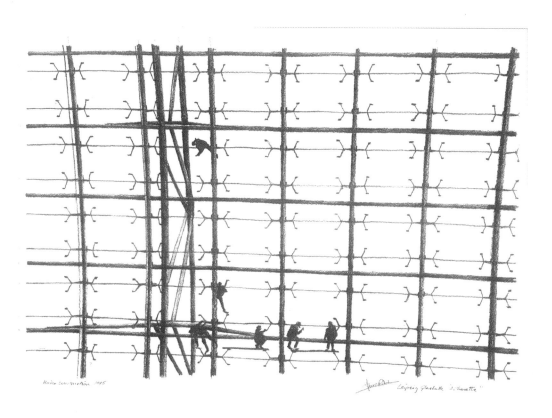

Hadin construction 1995

Leipzig Glashalle "Silhouette"

Transparent envelopes receive natural light with its continuously changing qualities; they modify it spectrally as it passes through glass. Transparency is rarely an architectural composition of light but a dynamic saturation of space which nearly always requires shading to control of the quantity of sunlight. Consequently, the design of the shading will create the external architectural expression, even the essence of the architecture. Transparency has no light, translucency is for shadows and opacity is rendered light.

Stockley Park research offices, stainless steel solar shading
– *photo Ian Ritchie*

Three Stones

These three stones carry
the three shadows of time.
The landscape is still and I'm
drawing shadows, three.

A setting and view
across to Galway Bay,
the ruined Corcomroe Abbey,
in Mayo, Slieve Carn dark blue.

I can hear the trace
of sound through shaded space,
feel the carrier, air, on my face
caressing the stones' surface.

Sensual wind singing,
stones frame a bird in flight
in earth's diurnal rhythm of light,
cosmic night stirring.

Remote, balanced, and time-
resisting rain, sun and wind while
giving a wonderful sense of exile
within the space of three lime
stones or, is it four?

Cromlech, Poulaphuca, The Burren, Ireland, from the northwest
– *drawing Ian Ritchie*

Published in 2023 by Unicorn
an imprint of
Unicorn Publishing Group
Charleston Studio
Meadow Business Centre
Lewes BN8 5RW
www.unicornpublishing.org

✳ ritchie
 studio

COVER IMAGE
Alba di Milano, light monument
winning concept for
the millennium
– etching Ian Ritchie

PAGE 5
Triple Spout by William Pye,
courtesy of the artist
– photo Douglas Atfield

Every effort has been made to trace
copyright holders and to obtain their
permission for the use of copyrighted
material. The publisher apologises for any
errors or omissions and would be grateful to
be notified of any corrections that should be
incorporated in future reprints or editions
of this book.

ISBN 978-1-911397-75-5
10 9 8 7 6 5 4 3 2 1

Design by corvo-uk.com
Printed in Riga by Finetone Ltd